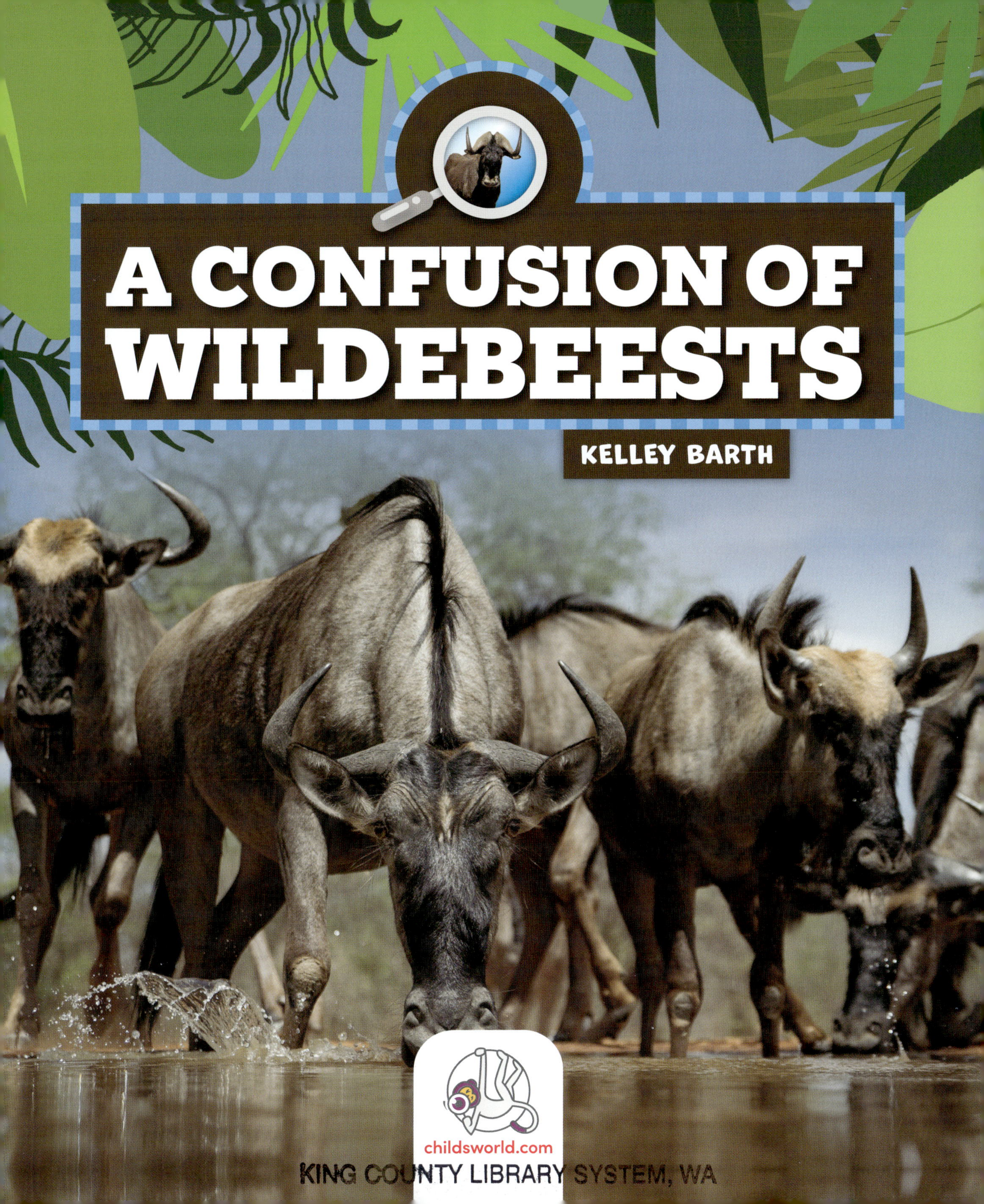

A CONFUSION OF WILDEBEESTS

KELLEY BARTH

childsworld.com

Published by The Child's World®
800-599-READ • www.childsworld.com

Photography Credits
page 1: ©Nick Dale/500px/Getty Images; page 1: ©Anastasiia Verych/Shutterstock; page 1: ©Villiers Steyn/Shutterstock; page 5: ©Keith Lewis Hull England/Getty Images; page 11: ©Scott Canning/Getty Images; page 13: ©Manoj Shah/Getty Images; page 15: ©Torleif Svensson/Getty Images; page 17: ©Anup Shah/Getty Images; page 18: ©Paul Souders/Getty Images; page 20: ©Anna-Carina Nagel/Getty Images; © Pauline St. Denis/Corbis/VCG/Getty Images

ISBN Information
9781503885035 (Reinforced Library Binding)
9781503885813 (Portable Document Format)
9781503886452 (Online Multi-user eBook)
9781503887091 (Electronic Publication)

LCCN 2023937383

Printed in the United States of America

Kelley Barth is a former children's librarian who loves connecting with young people over stories and books. When she isn't busy writing, she enjoys reading, hiking, crafting, and exploring national parks. She lives in Minnesota with her husband and their dog.

TABLE OF CONTENTS

CHAPTER 1

Meet the Confusion

Thousands of wildebeests gather on the bank of Africa's Mara River. It's a steep jump down into the water. They stomp nervously and toss their horned heads. The water is dangerous. It could easily sweep them away. Crocodiles could be hiding in it. One wildebeest takes the plunge. She leaps down and starts swimming, holding her head above the surface. Another follows her. Soon, the river is full of wildebeests. The wildebeests climb out on the other side and shake the water off their coats. They made it! In several months they'll have to make the dangerous crossing back again in search of food. But for now, they're safe.

Wildebeests get a running start and leap into the river.

Wildebeests are a type of antelope. They have large heads and thin legs. Wildebeests have dark manes and long, hairy tails. Both male and female wildebeests have horns like a cow. Males have longer horns.

Wildebeest means "wild beast." Gnu (NEW) is another name for a wildebeest. This is because the noise they make sounds like "ga-noo!" A **herd** of wildebeests is called a confusion. A confusion can have up to 10,000 wildebeests! But most confusions have only around 10 animals.

Wildebeest Size Comparison

The blue wildebeest is 55–60 inches (140–152 centimeters) tall and weighs between 510–605 pounds (230–275 kilograms).

A white-tailed deer stands up to 42 inches tall (106 cm) and can weigh as much as 400 pounds (180 kg).

CONFUSING!

Wildebeests are very noisy. So many animals live together that they can easily become confused. They can get lost or hurt. It looks confusing for anyone watching. This is why a group of wildebeests is called a confusion!

AFRICA

Atlantic Ocean

Indian Ocean

KEY

Where wildebeests live

Confusions of wildebeests live in southern and eastern Africa. They live in **savannas**, grasslands, and woodlands. Wildebeests live where there is lots of grass to eat. They stay close to water so they have plenty to drink.

There are two types of wildebeest. The blue wildebeest is more common. They are gray or brown and have black stripes on their shoulders. There are around 1.5 million blue wildebeests in the wild.

The black wildebeest is smaller and dark brown or black. They have curved horns and white tails. Years ago, too many people hunted black wildebeests. They almost became **extinct**. Most black wildebeests now live on farms or animal **reserves**. But no matter where they live, all wildebeests travel, eat, and sleep in confusions.

CHAPTER 2

All in the Family

Wildebeests **mate** once a year. Males compete for the right to mate with females. They fight and headbutt each other. The male wildebeest who wins gets to mate with the most females.

Eight months later, wildebeest babies are born. Baby wildebeests are called calves. Almost all calves in a confusion are born within the same two or three weeks. Wildebeests give birth standing in the middle of the herd. The herd helps protect the mother and new calf from **predators**.

Calves can stand and walk minutes after they are born. Soon, they are on the move with their confusion. Wildebeest calves drink their mother's milk for up to nine months. After ten days, they also start eating grass. Male wildebeests leave their mothers after about one year.

Calves are born without horns. Their horns are full-grown by the time they are five years old.

Who's in Charge?

Confusions are mostly made of female wildebeests and their calves. Female wildebeests stay in the same herd with their mothers. Young male wildebeests form their own confusions, called **bachelor** herds. But when they're about four or five years old, they separate from the group. Older male wildebeests don't live in herds. Instead they have **territories**.

Male wildebeests protect their territory. They leave their **dung** around to warn other animals to stay away. Males will also fight over territories. They hit the ground with their hooves and toss their horns. This warns other male wildebeests to stay away. During the breeding season, this helps them to protect the females they want to mate with.

A male wildebeest's horns can grow up to 2.7 feet (83 cm) long.

Confusions face many dangers. Predators hunt calves because they are slower than adult wildebeests. Lions, hyenas, leopards, cheetahs, and African wild dogs eat wildebeests. Crocodiles attack wildebeests when they get close to water. The confusion stays together for protection. They sleep in rows on the ground at night to stay safe from predators.

When they sense danger, wildebeests make loud calls. They stomp on the ground. The noise scares off predators. It also warns other wildebeests of danger. If a predator attacks, the confusion will run away. They can run 50 miles (80 kilometers) per hour. Sometimes a **stampede** happens if a predator attacks and the wildebeests start to run.

Wildebeests are fast, but cheetahs are faster. They can easily catch a lost or injured wildebeest.

CHAPTER 4

What Makes Confusions Unique?

Wildebeest confusions **migrate** every year. This means they move from one place to another. They travel in a big loop that can sometimes equal more than 1,000 miles (1,609 km). They migrate to find water to drink and green grass to eat. The area wildebeests live in has a dry season and a rainy season. When it becomes too hot and dry, the confusion must move. This is called the Serengeti Migration.

More than one million wildebeests migrate each year. Smaller confusions join together into larger groups, or superherds. There are so many wildebeests that the ground shakes when they walk. Migration is a dangerous time. Every year, thousands of wildebeests die on their journey. Predators will eat some. Others drown crossing rivers. Some are crushed in stampedes.

Wildebeests and zebras have different strengths. Zebras can see better than wildebeests, and wildebeests can hear and smell better than zebras.

ANIMAL FRIENDS

A confusion of wildebeests sometimes lives with other animals, such as zebras. Living together is helpful for both animals. Zebras eat the tops of grasses. This makes it easier for wildebeests to eat the tasty bottom layer. Zebras also have very good eyesight. They often spot predators first. Zebras act as an early warning system. This helps confusions stay safe.

CHAPTER 5

Why Confusions Matter

Every year, many people travel to Africa to watch the Serengeti Migration. They hire local guides to show them where to watch the wildebeests. Some people hike or drive into the wilderness. People want to watch the confusions cross rivers, like the Mara River.

But this migration is in danger. Human activity is causing weather patterns to change. This makes rivers move faster and have more water. More wildebeests die trying to cross. People build fences and roads that interrupt the migration path. Weather changes also make it harder for confusions to find enough food. Some groups are trying to protect the migrations. They are protecting certain areas for wildebeest confusions on their long migration.

People come from all over the world to watch the wildebeest migration.

Confusions of wildebeests are important. They help keep other plants and animals in their environment healthy. Wildebeests eat lots of grass. This helps other animals, such as gazelles, reach their favorite foods on the ground. Wildebeests also serve as food to keep predators alive. Even wildebeest dung is important! It enriches the ground and helps the grasslands grow as wildebeests migrate. Wildebeests take a big journey every year and have a big effect on the environment.

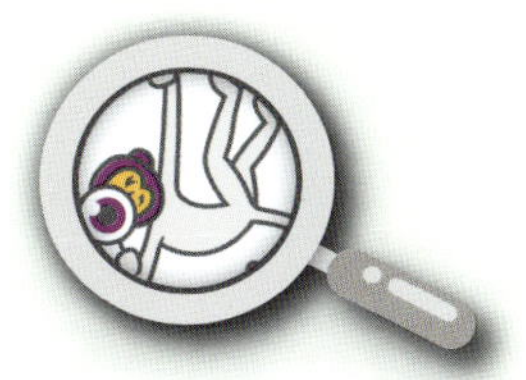

Wonder More

Wondering about New Information

What new information did you learn about wildebeest confusions? Write down three new facts that you learned. Did this information surprise you? Why or why not?

Wondering How It Matters

Why do confusions migrate? Describe what you might see, hear, and feel if you saw a confusion during its migration.

Wondering Why

The black wildebeest is endangered. They only live on farms and protected animal reserves. What can you do to help endangered animals?

Ways to Keep Wondering

After reading this book, what questions do you still have about confusions of wildebeests? What can you do to learn more about them?

Travel like a Wildebeest

Wildebeests are known for their large migrations. Sometimes they travel in a big loop that equals more than 1,000 miles (1,609 km). Where would you end up if you traveled that far? How would you get there?

What you Need:

- An atlas or map
- A ruler
- A pencil

Steps to Take:

1. Find where you live on a map. Draw a dot to mark it.
2. Use the map's distance scale to find out how far 1,000 miles (1,609 km) is and mark that on your ruler.
3. Use your ruler to find out how far away 1,000 miles (1,609 km) is from where you live. Try drawing out your travel path in different directions. Where do you end up? Choose one location.
4. How would you get to this location? Would you take a car? A bus? A plane? A boat? Do you think you could walk that far like a wildebeest?

Glossary

bachelor (BATCH-uh-lur) A bachelor is a male human or animal who does not have a partner.

dung (DUNG) Dung is animal waste.

extinct (ek-STINGKT) Extinct animals, plants, or other living things have completely disappeared from Earth.

herd (HURD) A herd is a large group of animals that live and travel together.

mate (MAYT) When animals mate, they join together to produce offspring.

migrate (MY-grayt) When animals migrate, they move from one place to another.

predators (PREH-duh-tuhrs) Predators are animals that hunt other animals for food.

reserves (ruh-ZURVZ) Reserves are pieces of land set aside to protect plants and animals.

savannas (suh-VAN-uhz) Savannas are large grasslands with few trees.

stampede (stam-PEED) A stampede is a large rush of scared animals.

territories (TAYR-ih-tor-eez) Territories are the areas of land that an animal or group lives on or defends.

Find Out More

In the Library

Emminizer, Theresa. *Wandering Wildebeests.* New York, NY: PowerKids Press, 2021.

Nelson, Penelope. *Wildebeests.* Minneapolis, MN: Bullfrog Books, 2020.

Unwin, Mike. *Migration: Incredible Animal Journeys.* New York, NY: Bloomsbury, 2019.

On the Web

Visit our website for links about wildebeest confusions:
childsworld.com/links

Note to Parents, Caregivers, Teachers, and Librarians: We routinely verify our web links to make sure they are safe and active sites. So encourage your readers to check them out!

Index